AN EXORCISTS CA

BIOGRAPHY OF FATHER GABR̶̶̶̶ ̶̶̶̶̶̶̶̶

LUCA LORENZO

FOREWARD BY BEAUTY SUNNY

Acknowledgements

Writing a book is a labor of love that involves the contributions and support of countless individuals, without whom this endeavor would have been impossible. As I pen down the acknowledgments for "An Exorcist Calling: Biography of Father Gabriele Amorth," I am overwhelmed with gratitude for the many people who have played an integral role in bringing this project to fruition.

First and foremost, I want to express my deepest appreciation to Father Gabriele Amorth, whose life and work have been the source of inspiration for this biography. His unwavering dedication to the ministry of exorcism and his remarkable journey in the service of the Church have left an indelible mark on the world. It was a privilege to research and share his story with the world.

My gratitude extends to the Amorth family for their openness and generosity in sharing personal anecdotes, photographs, and insights into Father Gabriele's life. Your willingness to provide access to his personal archives was instrumental in capturing the essence of his character and mission.

I am indebted to the countless individuals who graciously offered their time and expertise in helping me gather information and resources for this book. Special thanks to Florence Augustine and Alberto Sagasta for their invaluable interviews and research assistance.

I must acknowledge the guidance and encouragement of my literary agent and my editor. Your expert guidance and constructive feedback were instrumental in shaping this narrative into its final form.

I extend my heartfelt thanks to everyone who were involved in one way or another during the course of this project for your unwavering support throughout the publishing process and for believing in this project.

This journey wouldn't have been possible without the unyielding support of my family and friends. Your patience, encouragement, and understanding during long hours of research and writing are deeply appreciated.

I want to thank my readers, whose interest in Father Gabriele's life and work gives meaning to the words on these pages. Your curiosity and engagement are the ultimate reward for an author.

Finally, I offer my gratitude to the countless individuals who are part of Father Gabriele's global network of exorcists, scholars, and devoted followers. Your commitment to this important ministry is a testament to the enduring impact of his life's work.

In closing, this book stands as a testament to the power of collaboration, dedication, and faith. I am humbled and honored to have been entrusted with the task of sharing Father Gabriele Amorth's extraordinary journey with the world.

With deepest appreciation,

Luca Lorenzo

Table of Contents

INTRODUCTION

THE LIFE OF FATHER GABRIELE AMORTH

Father Gabriele Amorth was a prominent figure in the world of exorcism and a renowned Catholic priest. Born on May 1, 1925, in Modena, Italy, he dedicated his life to the service of the Church and became one of the most recognized exorcists in modern times. Amorth's journey into the world of exorcism began when he joined the Society of St. Paul, a Catholic religious congregation, and was ordained a priest in 1954.

Throughout his life, Father Gabriele Amorth held various roles within the Catholic Church, but it was his work as an exorcist that made him widely known. He served as the chief exorcist of the Diocese of Rome for many years, carrying out thousands of exorcisms during his career. His experiences and insights into the spiritual realm made him a sought-after expert in the field.

Amorth authored several books, including "An Exorcist Tells His Story" and "An Exorcist: More

Stories." In these books, he shared his experiences, beliefs, and the challenges he faced while performing exorcisms. He firmly believed in the reality of demonic possession and the need for trained exorcists to combat it.

Father Gabriele Amorth's dedication to his work extended beyond the confines of the Church. He was a vocal advocate for the importance of exorcism in addressing spiritual afflictions. He also expressed concerns about the increasing influence of the occult and the weakening of faith in society.

Amorth passed away on September 16, 2016, leaving behind a legacy of commitment to his faith and a deep understanding of the spiritual battles he fought throughout his life. His work continues to influence discussions about exorcism and the supernatural within the.

Catholic Church and beyond. Father Gabriele Amorth's life serves as a testament to his unwavering belief in the power of faith and the constant struggle between good and evil in the spiritual realm.

CHAPTER ONE

EARLY YEARS: FROM MILAN TO ROME

Gabriele Amorth's early years, from his birth in Modena, Italy, on May 1, 1925, to his eventual move to Rome, played a significant role in shaping his life and career. After his birth in Modena, he moved to Milan, where he received his education. It was during his time in Milan that he attended a Jesuit school, an experience that likely had a profound impact on his spiritual development.

His journey towards the priesthood began when he entered the seminary, a decision that marked a crucial turning point in his life. After years of theological studies and spiritual formation, Amorth was ordained as a Catholic priest in 1954. This marked the start of his formal ministry within the Church.

However, it was in Rome that Gabriele Amorth's life took a distinct path. In 1986, he joined the Congregation for the Doctrine of the Faith in Rome.

This congregation plays a central role in matters of Catholic doctrine and theology, including issues related to exorcism and demonic possession. It was within this context that Amorth's involvement in exorcism work began to gain prominence.

Amorth's relocation to Rome also positioned him to become the chief exorcist for the Diocese of Rome, a role that he would hold for many years. In this capacity, he conducted countless exorcisms, earning a reputation as one of the most experienced and dedicated exorcists in the Catholic Church.

Gabriele Amorth's journey from Milan to Rome marked the trajectory of his life towards his vocation as a priest and ultimately as a renowned exorcist. His early years in Milan and his later service in the heart of the Catholic Church in Rome were pivotal in shaping his career and his enduring legacy in the realm of spiritual warfare and exorcism.

CHAPTER TWO

THE SEMINARY AND PRIESTHOOD

Gabriele Amorth's seminary and priesthood were foundational to his later career as a prominent exorcist within the Catholic Church in these aspects:

1. Seminary Education:

Gabriele Amorth's path toward priesthood was marked by his dedicated seminary education. He embarked on the standard journey followed by those aspiring to become Catholic priests. His educational journey took him to the renowned Pontifical Gregorian University in Rome, which is highly respected for its focus on theology and philosophy. Within the seminary's hallowed halls, Amorth underwent rigorous training in various aspects of Catholicism, including an in-depth study of Catholic doctrine, liturgical practices, and the art of pastoral care. This foundational education played a crucial role in shaping his future as a priest and exorcist.

2. Spiritual Formation:

Amorth embarked on a demanding and transformative journey as he prepared for the sacred responsibilities of priesthood. The process was characterized by a rigorous spiritual formation that encompassed various essential components.

First and foremost,he prayed daily as daily prayer forms the cornerstone of a seminarian's life. He engaged in a structured routine of prayer, which not only deepened his personal connection with God but also fostered a sense of discipline and devotion. Through regular prayer, he learnt to draw strength and guidance from his faith, which was fundamental for his future role as a spiritual leader.

He actively participated in Mass as this is another pivotal aspect of his formation. Attending Mass daily enabled him to immerse himself in the liturgical traditions of the Church. It instilled a profound understanding of the sacraments and the Eucharist, which are central to the priestly ministry. Through this participation, he became intimately familiar with the rituals and rites he would one day administer to the faithful.

Additionally, spiritual direction plays a crucial role in a seminarian's journey. During this process, he received guidance and mentorship from experienced priests or spiritual directors. These mentors helped him navigate the complexities of their faith, offering insights into theological matters, moral dilemmas, and the practical aspects of pastoral care. Through such personalized guidance, he developed a deeper understanding of his vocation and the pastoral challenges he would face.

This period of formation was indispensable in cultivating a profound spiritual life for Amorth. It equiped him with the knowledge, faith, and resilience needed to confront the multifaceted demands of priesthood. He did not only learn to nourish his own soul but also to guide and support the spiritual growth of his future congregations. Ultimately, the rigorous process of spiritual formation prepared him for the immense responsibilities and sacred duties that come with priesthood, ensuring that he was well-prepared to serve the Church and its faithful.

3. Ordination:

In 1954, Gabriele Amorth's ordination as a Catholic priest marked a significant milestone in his life and the official beginning of his ministerial career within the Catholic Church. Following the completion of his theological studies and meeting the rigorous requirements set by the Church, he was granted the authority to serve as a priest. This sacred ordination not only represented a personal commitment to his faith but also signified his dedication to the spiritual well-being of the Catholic community.

As a Catholic priest, Gabriele Amorth was responsible for a range of pastoral duties, including celebrating Mass, administering sacraments, providing spiritual guidance and counsel to parishioners, and participating in various religious ceremonies. It was during this period that he underwent further training and gained practical experience in the responsibilities and obligations of a Catholic clergyman.

Little did anyone know at the time that Gabriele Amorth's journey as a priest would eventually lead him to become one of the most well-known and respected exorcists in the Catholic Church. His lifelong commitment to the Church and his dedication to the ministry would eventually bring him to the forefront of the Church's battle against demonic forces, solidifying his legacy as a prominent figure in the world of exorcism and spiritual warfare.

4. Parish Ministry:

After Father Gabriele Amorth's ordination as a Catholic priest, he embarked on a journey of service within various parishes. In these roles, he took on significant responsibilities, playing a vital role in the spiritual lives of the communities he served.

Celebrating Mass: As a priest, Father Amorth regularly celebrated the Mass, a central act of worship in the Catholic faith. This involved leading the congregation in prayer, consecrating the Eucharist, and delivering sermons that provided guidance and inspiration to the faithful. Through the repetition of this sacred ritual, he honed his skills in conveying the teachings of the Church and deepening his connection with the congregation.

Administering Sacraments: He was responsible for administering the sacraments, which are essential milestones in a Catholic's spiritual journey. This included performing baptisms, conducting weddings, and administering the sacrament of reconciliation (confession). These duties allowed Father Amorth to directly engage with parishioners during pivotal moments in their lives, providing them with guidance, support, and a sense of belonging within the Church.

Providing Spiritual Guidance: Father Amorth was a source of spiritual guidance and counsel for parishioners. People often turned to him for advice on matters of faith, morality, and personal challenges. Through these interactions, he developed his pastoral skills, learning to empathize with the diverse needs and struggles of his parishioners.

Building Community: Serving in various parishes gave Father Amorth the opportunity to foster a sense of community and unity among the faithful. He worked to bring people together through religious education, youth programs, and various parish activities, further enhancing his pastoral abilities.

Continual Learning: Throughout his service in different parishes, Father Amorth continued to deepen his theological knowledge and understanding of the Catholic Church's teachings. He pursued additional studies by attending workshops and conferences to stay informed about developments in theology and pastoral care.

Father Gabriele Amorth's experiences in various parishes after his ordination were pivotal for his development as a priest. These roles allowed him to cultivate his pastoral skills, strengthen his connection with the Church community, and provide spiritual guidance to the faithful. Such experiences undoubtedly shaped his future path, including his well-known work in the field of exorcism and demonology.

5. Appointment as an Exorcist:

Exorcists like Amorth play a unique and crucial role in the Catholic Church. They are tasked with performing exorcisms, a ritualistic practice aimed at expelling evil spirits or demons from individuals who are believed to be possessed. This responsibility requires a deep understanding of theology, demonology, and the liturgical procedures associated with exorcism.

Amorth's journey into this role involved rigorous training and mentorship to prepare him for the challenges he would face. Dealing with cases of alleged possession can be emotionally and spiritually taxing, as it involves confronting the forces of evil in a very direct way. Exorcists must possess unwavering faith, compassion, and a strong commitment to helping those in need, all while adhering to strict protocols established by the Church.

Amorth's unique path as an exorcist not only showcased his dedication to his faith but also highlighted the church's recognition of the importance of addressing spiritual and supernatural phenomena within the context of modern Catholicism. His work shed light on the enduring belief in the existence of evil forces and the need for individuals within the Church who are trained and willing to combat them in the name of faith and healing.

6. Ongoing Formation:

As an exorcist, Father Gabriele Amorth underwent extensive training and preparation in the field of exorcism and demonology. Here are some key aspects of his training:

Studying the Rituale Romanum: The Rituale Romanum, also known as the Roman Ritual, is the official liturgical book for conducting exorcisms within the Catholic Church. Father Amorth studied this text extensively to understand the prescribed prayers, rituals, and procedures for exorcisms. It serves as a guide for performing the rite of exorcism in accordance with the Church's teachings.

Theological Education: Before becoming an exorcist, individuals typically undergo theological education and training within the Catholic Church. This education would provide a strong foundation in Catholic doctrine, theology, and the understanding of evil and demonic possession from a religious perspective.

Mentorship and Practical Experience: Father Amorth worked closely with experienced exorcists who served as mentors. Learning from seasoned practitioners is crucial in this field, as it allows aspiring exorcists to observe and participate in actual exorcism rituals and gain practical insights into dealing with cases of possession or oppression.

Psychological and Medical Assessment: Exorcists often receive training in psychological and medical assessment to ensure that cases of apparent possession are carefully evaluated. Many cases that initially appear to be possession have underlying psychological or medical explanations, and it's essential to distinguish between these issues.

Continual Learning and Updates: The field of exorcism and demonology is constantly evolving, and new challenges and manifestations of evil may arise. Exorcists, including Father Amorth, engaged in continual learning and updates to stay informed about emerging issues and refine their practices.

Spiritual Preparation: Spiritual preparation is a fundamental aspect of an exorcist's training. This involves deepening one's personal spirituality, prayer life, and relationship with God to draw strength and guidance when confronting malevolent forces.

Father Amorth's training as an exorcist encompassed a comprehensive understanding of the Rituale Romanum, theological education, mentorship, practical experience, psychological and medical assessment, continual learning, and spiritual preparation. This combination of knowledge and spiritual grounding is essential for those who engage in the ministry of exorcism within the Catholic Church.

7. International Recognition:

Gabriele Amorth's expertise in exorcism indeed gained significant recognition over the years, solidifying his status as a prominent figure within the Catholic Church. His dedication to the practice of exorcism went beyond performing rituals; he actively engaged in educating others and raising awareness about this spiritual aspect of the Church.

Amorth's contributions were multifaceted. He conducted seminars and training sessions, not only for fellow priests but also for interested individuals seeking to understand the intricacies of exorcism. Through these events, he shared his knowledge, experiences, and insights, equipping others with the tools to address cases of possession and spiritual affliction.

In addition to his live teachings, Amorth also spoke at conferences and religious gatherings worldwide. His speeches often delved into the theological and practical aspects of exorcism, shedding light on its relevance in contemporary society. These appearances further amplified his influence and helped foster a greater understanding of the Church's role in combating spiritual maladies.

Amorth's commitment to spreading awareness extended to the written word. He authored several books on the subject of exorcism, offering readers a deeper understanding of the phenomenon and its significance within the Catholic faith. His books, which included detailed case studies and theological insights, became valuable resources for both scholars and the general public.

Through interviews with various media outlets, Amorth shared his wisdom and experiences, reaching an even broader audience. His candid discussions on exorcism, possession, and the battle against evil forces helped demystify these subjects and fostered a more informed discourse.

In sum, Gabriele Amorth's work in the field of exorcism transcended mere practice; it encompassed education, public speaking, and literary contributions. His efforts played a pivotal role in increasing awareness of exorcism within the Catholic Church and beyond, leaving a lasting legacy in the realm of spiritual warfare and faith.

CHAPTER THREE

VATICAN CITY: A NEW BEGINNING

Father Amorth's journey towards becoming an exorcist began when he joined the Society of St. Paul in 1947. He was ordained as a priest in 1954. Later, he became a member of the Congregation for the Doctrine of the Faith and the Vatican's chief exorcist, a position he held for many years.

He was indeed a well-known Italian priest and exorcist who dedicated his life to the service of the Catholic Church. He gained prominence for his extensive work in the field of exorcism, particularly during his time at the Vatican.

In this role, he was responsible for evaluating and performing exorcisms on individuals believed to be possessed by evil spirits.

During his tenure as a member of the Congregation for the Doctrine of the Faith and the Vatican's chief exorcist, he played a pivotal role in addressing matters related to the Catholic Church's teachings and beliefs. Here are some key aspects of what happened during those years:

Doctrinal Matters: As a member of the Congregation for the Doctrine of the Faith, he was involved in discussions and decisions concerning matters of doctrine, theology, and church teachings. This congregation is responsible for safeguarding the faith's integrity and ensuring that the Church's teachings are consistent with its tradition.

Exorcism Ministry: Serving as the Vatican's chief exorcist, he was responsible for performing exorcisms and overseeing the Church's efforts to combat demonic possession and spiritual affliction. This role required extensive knowledge of ritualistic practices, prayers, and the discernment of genuine cases from psychological or medical conditions.

Training and Guidance: He was involved in training and mentoring other priests who were learning the art of exorcism. This included teaching them the proper procedures, rituals, and prayers to follow when conducting exorcisms, as well as providing guidance on how to handle difficult cases.

Investigations and Assessments: During his tenure, he was involved in assessing cases of alleged possession or supernatural phenomena, determining whether they warranted an exorcism, or if there were alternative explanations such as mental illness or psychological issues.

Spiritual Counseling: Apart from exorcisms, he provided spiritual counseling and support to individuals seeking relief from spiritual distress. This would have included listening to their concerns, offering prayers, and helping them find solace in their faith.

Controversies and Public Attention: It's worth noting that individuals in such a high-profile role often attract public attention and sometimes controversy. He may have been involved in addressing media inquiries and public perceptions surrounding exorcism and the Catholic Church's stance on supernatural phenomena.

Those years were marked by a combination of theological discussions, spiritual ministry, and dealing with various challenges related to the practice of exorcism within the Catholic Church.

Father Gabriele Amorth was one of the most prominent exorcists in the Catholic Church. He performed thousands of exorcisms throughout his career, often in Vatican City. His experiences in performing these exorcisms contributed to his reputation.

Father Amorth held the position of Chief Exorcist of the Diocese of Rome, which encompasses Vatican City. In this role, he was responsible for addressing cases of possession and conducting exorcisms for those believed to be afflicted by demonic forces.

CHAPTER FOUR

THE VATICAN'S CHIEF EXORCIST

Father Gabriele Amorth was a renowned figure in the Catholic Church, often referred to as "The Vatican's Chief Exorcist." Amorth's fame primarily stemmed from his extensive experience in performing exorcisms and his outspoken beliefs in the reality of demonic possession.

Amorth became a priest in 1954 and later joined the Society of St. Paul, an order focused on using media to spread the Christian message. However, it was his role as an exorcist that brought him widespread recognition. He claimed to have conducted tens of thousands of exorcisms throughout his career, which spanned several decades. Amorth firmly believed that the devil was real and that exorcisms were a vital part of the Church's ministry.

In 1986, Father Amorth was part of the initiatives that founded the International Association of

Exorcists, an organization dedicated to promoting the practice of exorcism and providing support to priests involved in this ministry. He served as the president of this association until his retirement.

Father Amorth's views on exorcism were often controversial, as he maintained a firm belief in the existence of demonic possession and insisted that exorcisms were necessary to combat evil forces. He authored several books, including "An Exorcist Tells His Story" and "An Exorcist: More Stories," in which he shared his experiences and beliefs.

Despite facing skepticism and criticism from some quarters, Father Gabriele Amorth remained steadfast in his convictions and continued to perform exorcisms until his passing on September 16, 2016. He left behind a legacy as one of the most well-known and dedicated exorcists in the history of the Catholic Church, earning him the title "The Vatican's Chief Exorcist."

CHAPTER FIVE

BATTLING EVIL: FATHER AMORTH'S EXORCISMS

"Battling Evil: Father Amorth's Exorcisms" is a book written by Father Gabriele Amorth, a renowned Italian Roman Catholic priest and exorcist. Published in 2017, the book provides an in-depth look into Father Amorth's experiences as an exorcist and his views on the battle against evil spirits.

Father Amorth was one of the most prominent exorcists in the Catholic Church, having performed thousands of exorcisms throughout his career. In his book, he delves into the world of exorcisms, offering readers an insider's perspective on the spiritual warfare between good and evil. Here are some key aspects of the book:

- **Exorcism Cases:** Father Amorth recounts various exorcism cases he encountered during his long career. He shares detailed stories of individuals who believed they were possessed by demons and the intense exorcism rituals performed to free them from malevolent spirits.
- **Theological Insights:** The book also explores the theological aspects of exorcism. Father Amorth discusses the nature of evil, the existence of demons, and the role of the Church in confronting spiritual oppression.
- **Controversial Topics:** Father Amorth doesn't shy away from controversial topics. He addresses issues such as the influence of the occult, the rise in possession cases, and the challenges faced by exorcists in the modern world.
- **Spiritual Insights:** Throughout the book, Father Amorth provides spiritual insights into the battle against evil. He emphasizes the importance of faith, prayer, and the sacraments as tools to combat demonic forces.
- **Spiritual Warfare:** Father Amorth believed that exorcism was a form of spiritual warfare, and the book discusses his views

on the battle between good and evil. He argued that evil forces were very real and that exorcists played a crucial role in confronting and defeating them.

- **Critiques and Responses**: Father Amorth responds to critics of exorcism, both within and outside the Church. He defends the practice of exorcism as a legitimate and necessary ministry.
- **Impact on Popular Culture:** The book, along with Father Amorth's public persona, contributed to the fascination with exorcism in popular culture. It influenced movies, TV shows, and literature, further perpetuating the intrigue surrounding this topic.
- **Legacy**: The book serves as part of Father Amorth's legacy, as he passed away in 2016. It continues to inspire and inform those interested in the field of exorcism and spirituality.
- **Debate and Ongoing Discussions:** The book also serves as a point of reference for ongoing debates about the intersection of religion, psychology, and the supernatural. It raises questions about the nature of

possession and the role of exorcism in addressing mental health issues.

"Battling Evil: Father Amorth's Exorcisms" offers a comprehensive exploration of Father Gabriele Amorth's life, experiences, and beliefs as a prominent Catholic exorcist. It provides insight into the world of exorcism, spiritual warfare, and the ongoing debates surrounding these practices in the modern world.

It's important to note that the subject matter of exorcism is a matter of religious belief and is often met with skepticism and controversy. Father Amorth's book offers a unique perspective from someone who dedicated his life to this practice within the context of his Catholic faith. Readers should approach the book with an open mind and an understanding of its religious context.

CHAPTER SIX

THEOLOGY OF EXORCISM

Gabriele Amorth was a renowned Catholic priest and exorcist who held strong views on the theology of exorcism. His perspective was deeply rooted in traditional Catholic teachings and his extensive experience performing exorcisms. Amorth believed that exorcism was a legitimate and necessary practice within the Church, and his views can be summarized in several key points:

- **Spiritual Warfare**: Amorth viewed exorcism as a form of spiritual warfare, a battle against evil forces. He believed that demonic possession was a real and dangerous phenomenon, and exorcists were spiritual soldiers combating these dark forces on behalf of individuals in need.
- **The Reality of Evil:** Amorth emphasized the reality of evil spirits and their influence on human lives. He argued that evil entities

could attach themselves to individuals, leading to various forms of spiritual and psychological distress.

- **Faith and Prayer:** Amorth emphasized the importance of faith and prayer in the exorcism process. He believed that both the possessed individual and the exorcist needed strong faith to confront and expel evil spirits. Prayer, particularly the use of ancient rituals and prayers from the Church, played a central role in the exorcism ritual.

- **Collaboration with Medical Professionals:** While firmly rooted in the spiritual realm, Amorth acknowledged the importance of collaboration with medical and psychological professionals. He believed in the need to rule out any purely medical or psychological explanations for a person's condition before considering exorcism.

- **Exorcism as a Sacramental**: In Amorth's view, exorcism was a sacramental act of the Church. He saw it as an extension of the Church's mission to heal and save souls, and he adhered to the formal procedures outlined by the Church for conducting exorcisms.

- **Confidentiality and Discretion:** Amorth stressed the importance of maintaining confidentiality and discretion in cases of possession and exorcism. He believed that the identity and privacy of those seeking help should be protected.
- **Continuous Training:** Throughout his life, Amorth continued to study and train in the field of exorcism. He believed that exorcists should be well-prepared, spiritually strong, and knowledgeable about the evolving nature of evil and demonic tactics.

Gabriele Amorth's theology of exorcism revolved around the belief in the reality of evil spirits, the importance of faith and prayer, collaboration with medical professionals, and the adherence to the Church's sacramental rituals. His views were shaped by his experiences as an exorcist and his dedication to helping those afflicted by demonic forces.

CHAPTER SEVEN

CONTROVERSIES AND CRITICISMS

Father Gabriele Amorth was a Roman Catholic priest who gained notoriety for his involvement in exorcisms and his role as the chief exorcist of the Diocese of Rome. While many people believed in his work, there were also controversies and criticisms surrounding him:

1. **Lack of Scientific Evidence:** One of the main criticisms of Father Amorth's work was the absence of scientific evidence to support his claims of demonic possession and the effectiveness of exorcisms. Skeptics argued that the phenomena he attributed to possession could often be explained by medical or psychological conditions.

2. **Overreliance on Exorcism:** Critics contended that Father Amorth was too quick to diagnose individuals as possessed and relied too heavily

on exorcisms as a solution. They argued that this approach could be harmful to those suffering from mental or physical illnesses, as they might not receive proper medical care.

3. **Secrecy and Lack of Accountability:** Some critics accused Father Amorth and other exorcists of operating in secrecy, making it difficult to scrutinize their methods and outcomes. This lack of transparency raised concerns about potential abuses or misjudgments.

4. **Conflicting Theological Views:** Within the Catholic Church, there were differing theological views on the role of exorcism and demonic possession. Some theologians questioned whether the emphasis on exorcisms was in line with modern interpretations of Catholic doctrine.

5. **Pop Culture Influence:** Father Amorth's media presence and the popularity of movies and books on exorcisms, such as "The Exorcist," contributed to concerns that he may have been influenced by or contributed to sensationalism surrounding the topic.

6. **Controversial Statements:** Father Amorth made several controversial statements during his career, such as claiming that yoga and Harry

Potter were pathways to the devil. These remarks were met with criticism and skepticism from various quarters.

7. **Lack of Formal Training:** Some critics argued that Father Amorth, despite his long tenure as an exorcist, did not have formal psychological or psychiatric training, which they believed was necessary to differentiate between genuine cases of possession and mental health issues.

It's important to note that Father Amorth had a significant following and was supported by many within the Catholic Church who believed in the reality of demonic possession and the need for exorcisms. However, these controversies and criticisms illustrate the complex and polarizing nature of his work and beliefs.

CHAPTER EIGHT

A LIFE DEVOTED TO SPIRITUAL WARFARE

Father Gabriele Amorth was a Catholic priest and renowned exorcist who devoted his life to spiritual warfare, primarily through his work in performing exorcisms and battling demonic forces.

He passionately advocated for acknowledging the presence of evil forces and stressed the significance of having well-trained exorcists within the Catholic Church. His dedication to this cause was unwavering, as he believed that confronting the reality of evil was essential for spiritual well-being.

He worked tirelessly to raise awareness about the dangers associated with occult practices. He saw these practices as potential gateways for malevolent forces to infiltrate the lives of individuals and communities. His efforts included speaking at conferences, writing articles and books, and engaging in dialogues with fellow clergy and scholars.

Moreover, he emphasized the crucial role of spiritual discernment in safeguarding the faithful. He believed that a deep understanding of one's faith and the ability to distinguish between genuine spiritual experiences and deceptive influences were paramount. He promoted educational programs and resources within the Church to equip priests and laypeople with the tools needed for effective spiritual discernment.

His advocacy revolved around recognizing and combatting evil, strengthening the Church's ability to perform exorcisms, and educating believers about the perils of occult practices while emphasizing the importance of spiritual discernment as a shield against such threats. His work left a lasting impact on the Catholic Church's approach to these crucial issues.

He believed in the reality of demonic possession and dedicated his life to helping individuals he believed were afflicted by evil spirits. How Father Amorth performed exorcisms and battled demonic forces were through:

1. **Preparation and Assessment:** Father Amorth would begin by carefully assessing the person who sought his help. He would conduct interviews to determine whether the individual's symptoms were consistent with signs of possession. He also consulted with medical professionals to rule out any underlying medical or psychological conditions.

2. **Permission from the Church:** Exorcisms in the Catholic Church require special permission from a bishop. Father Amorth followed the Church's protocols and obtained the necessary authorization before performing exorcisms.

3. **Spiritual Preparation:** Before each exorcism, Father Amorth would engage in prayer and fasting to spiritually prepare himself for the battle against demonic forces. He believed that maintaining a strong faith and connection with God was essential in this work.

4. **Liturgical Rites:** Father Amorth followed the Roman Catholic Rite of Exorcism, which is a ritualized form of prayer and supplication to cast out demons. He would use prayers, holy water, and the sign of the cross during the exorcism.

5. **Authority and Command:** He firmly believed in the authority of the priest in the name of Jesus

Christ to command demons to leave the possessed person. He would directly address the demonic entity, demanding that it depart.

6. **Support from Assistants:** During exorcisms, Father Amorth often had one or more assistants to help restrain the possessed person, offer support, and join in prayer. This was important for both practical and spiritual reasons.

7. **Multiple Sessions:** Exorcisms were rarely a one-time event. Father Amorth understood that some cases required multiple sessions over an extended period before the individual was completely free from demonic influence.

8. **Continuous Prayer and Spiritual Guidance:** After the exorcism, Father Amorth would provide ongoing spiritual guidance and support to the person to help them maintain their spiritual well-being.

It's important to note that Father Amorth's methods and beliefs were rooted in his Catholic faith and the Church's teachings on exorcism. His work was often controversial and subject to skepticism from some quarters, but he remained steadfast in his conviction that demonic possession was a real phenomenon and that he was called to help those suffering from it.

Father Amorth and the International Association of Exorcists, an organization of Catholic priests dedicated to promoting and supporting the practice of exorcism worldwide.

The IAE is an organization of Catholic priests focused on the ministry of exorcism and providing support and training for priests involved in this practice. Father Amorth served as the honorary president of the IAE and was a driving force behind its activities.

Father Amorth conducted thousands of exorcisms throughout his career and authored several books on the subject, helping to raise awareness of the Catholic Church's continuing belief in the reality of demonic possession and the need for trained exorcists.

His contributions to the IAE and the field of exorcism have made him a well-known figure in the Catholic Church, even though he didn't co-found the organization itself.

Father Gabriele Amorth devoted his life to confronting the forces of evil and providing spiritual assistance to those in need through his ministry as an exorcist and his efforts to educate and advocate for the recognition of spiritual warfare within the Catholic Church.

CHAPTER NINE

INTERACTIONS WITH POPES AND CHURCH LEADERS

Father Gabriele Amorth was a prominent figure in the Catholic Church, particularly known for his work as an exorcist. He had interactions with several Popes and Church leaders during his lifetime. He had interactions with:

- **Pope Paul VI**: Father Gabriele Amorth, a renowned exorcist, commenced his career in the field of exorcism during the papacy of Pope Paul VI in the early 1960s. At that time, he operated discreetly, often working behind the scenes to assist individuals who were believed to be suffering from demonic possession or spiritual afflictions. His role extended beyond performing exorcisms; he also offered spiritual guidance and support to those experiencing these troubling phenomena.

Under Pope Paul VI's papacy, Father Amorth's work was instrumental in addressing cases of alleged demonic possession within the Catholic Church. He was a dedicated advocate for the practice of exorcism and worked tirelessly to raise awareness about the reality of evil spirits and the need for trained exorcists within the Church.

Throughout his career, Father Amorth's efforts contributed to the development of a greater understanding of exorcism and its role within the Church. He also authored several books on the subject, sharing his experiences and insights, which further illuminated the challenges and complexities of this unique ministry. His commitment to this work continued for decades, ultimately making him a prominent figure in the realm of exorcism and spiritual warfare.

- **Pope John Paul II:** Father Gabriele Amorth's interactions with Pope John Paul II indeed held great significance in the realm of exorcism and the Catholic Church. Their close relationship was rooted in their shared belief in the existence of evil forces and the need for spiritual intervention.

Father Amorth served as the chief exorcist of the Vatican for over two decades, making him one of the most prominent figures in the field of exorcism. His expertise and dedication to combating what he perceived as manifestations of evil led him to have frequent private audiences with Pope John Paul II.

During these meetings, Father Amorth and the Pope would engage in discussions about the challenges posed by the presence of evil in the world and the role of exorcism in confronting it. Their shared commitment to addressing spiritual afflictions and providing solace to those suffering from possession or spiritual distress cemented their bond.

Pope John Paul II, known for his strong faith and spiritual convictions, supported Father Amorth's work and recognized the importance of exorcism within the Catholic Church. This collaboration between the Pope and the chief exorcist underscored the Church's acknowledgment of the reality of evil forces and its commitment to confronting them through prayer and spiritual healing.

Father Amorth's close relationship with Pope John Paul II was marked by their shared beliefs and their dedication to addressing the presence of evil in the world. Their discussions and collaboration on matters related to exorcism served as a testament to their commitment to spiritual healing and the protection of the faithful.

- **Pope Benedict XVI:** Father Gabriele Amorth, indeed continued his work during Pope Benedict XVI's papacy. He was a prominent figure within the Catholic Church and remained dedicated to his role as an exorcist throughout this period. Father Amorth's commitment to performing exorcisms and offering insights into the Church's stance on demonic possession and evil was unwavering.

During Pope Benedict XVI's papacy, which began in 2005 and ended in 2013, Father Amorth continued to be one of the Church's most respected and active exorcists. He conducted numerous exorcisms, and his experiences dealing with cases of alleged demonic possession garnered significant attention from both within and outside the Church. Father Amorth often emphasized the reality of evil and the importance of spiritual warfare, as he believed that the battle against demonic forces was ongoing and required vigilance.

Father Amorth's work not only involved performing exorcisms but also educating others about the Church's teachings on this subject. He authored books and articles that aimed to shed light on the nature of demonic possession and how the Church approached it. His writings and public statements provided valuable insights into the Church's views, emphasizing the need for discernment and pastoral care when dealing with individuals who believed they were afflicted by evil spirits.

Throughout his time under Pope Benedict XVI's leadership, Father Amorth's dedication to his role as an exorcist contributed to the ongoing dialogue within the Catholic Church about the supernatural and the role of exorcism in confronting evil. His legacy endures as a symbol of the Church's commitment to addressing spiritual and supernatural issues, even in the modern world.

- **Pope Francis**: Father Gabriele Amorth held critical views of Pope Francis, particularly regarding the Pope's approach to exorcisms and his emphasis on mercy rather than the battle against evil. Father Amorth believed in a more traditional and assertive approach to exorcism, often expressing concerns that Pope Francis was not taking the threat of the devil and demonic possession seriously enough.

Despite these differences in perspective, Pope Francis acknowledged the importance of exorcism and the need for trained exorcists within the Church. While he may have a more inclusive and compassionate stance on many issues, Pope Francis recognized that the battle against evil, including the reality of demonic possession, remains a significant aspect of the Church's mission. He affirmed the need for proper training and discernment in identifying cases of possession and ensuring that they are treated with the utmost care and respect.

In 2014, Pope Francis officially recognized the International Association of Exorcists, which brought together Catholic priests trained in exorcism from various countries. This recognition indicated his awareness of the role of exorcists within the Church and his support for their work.

While there were differences in perspective between Father Amorth and Pope Francis, the latter acknowledged the importance of exorcism and the necessity of having trained individuals within the Church to address cases of demonic possession, emphasizing the need for both mercy and spiritual discernment in dealing with these challenging situations.

- **Other Church Leaders**: Father Amorth, best known for his interactions with Popes, had a significant impact beyond his involvement with the Vatican. He indeed had interactions with various Church leaders and bishops who sought his expertise in matters of exorcism. These interactions extended to several aspects:

1. **Consultations on Alleged Demonic Possession:** Father Amorth was frequently consulted by priests, bishops, and even dioceses worldwide when dealing with cases of alleged demonic possession. His reputation as an experienced exorcist led many to seek his guidance in assessing the authenticity of such cases and determining the appropriate course of action. He was known for his meticulous approach, ensuring that the Church's response was both compassionate and in line with established protocols.

2. **Training of New Exorcists:** Father Amorth played a crucial role in the training of new exorcists. Recognizing the need for more qualified individuals to carry out the Church's ministry of exorcism, he took it upon himself to

impart his knowledge and experience to the next generation. He conducted workshops, seminars, and training sessions to educate priests on the intricacies of exorcism, emphasizing the importance of discernment and spiritual discernment.

3. **Establishing Guidelines and Protocols:** Father Amorth's interactions with Church leaders and bishops also contributed to the development and refinement of guidelines and protocols for conducting exorcisms. His insights and experiences informed discussions within the Church about how to approach cases of demonic possession, ensuring that the process was conducted with due care and respect for the individuals involved.

4. **Raising Awareness:** Through his interactions with Church leaders and the broader religious community, Father Amorth played a role in raising awareness about the reality of demonic possession and the importance of trained exorcists. He emphasized that exorcism was not a subject of mere superstition but a valid and essential ministry within the Church.

Father Amorth's interactions with Church leaders and bishops extended far beyond his connections with Popes. He was a respected figure in the realm of exorcism, sought after for his expertise, and instrumental in shaping the Church's approach to this important aspect of its ministry. His legacy continues to influence the practice of exorcism and spiritual discernment within the Catholic Church.

Throughout his life, Father Gabriele Amorth remained dedicated to his calling as an exorcist and engaged in public discussions about the reality of evil and the need for exorcism within the Catholic Church. His interactions with Popes and Church leaders were instrumental in bringing attention to the practice of exorcism and its role within the Church.

CHAPTER TEN

INSIGHTS INTO DEMONIC POSSESSION

Father Gabriele Amorth's firm belief in the reality of demonic possession was deeply rooted in his Catholic faith and his experiences as a practicing exorcist. His various perspectives inclded:

- **Spiritual Perspective:** Father Amorth viewed demonic possession as a spiritual phenomenon rather than a psychological or medical one. He believed that individuals could become vessels for malevolent entities, allowing evil spirits or demons to take control of their bodies and minds.
- **Biblical Foundation:** His belief in demonic possession was based on the teachings of the Bible, which contains numerous references to demoniacs and exorcisms performed by Jesus and his disciples. He saw these biblical accounts as evidence of the existence of evil spirits.

- **Spiritual Warfare:** Father Amorth considered exorcism as a form of spiritual warfare. In his view, the battle against demonic possession was a fundamental aspect of the Christian faith. He believed that the devil and his minions actively sought to corrupt and harm humanity.
- **Symptoms of Possession:** According to Father Amorth, the symptoms of demonic possession could include extreme personality changes, speaking in languages unknown to the possessed individual, supernatural strength, aversion to religious symbols or objects, and displays of aggression or violence.
- **Exorcism as a Sacramental:** In Catholicism, exorcism is regarded as a sacramental—a sacred ritual that calls upon the power of God to cast out demons. Father Amorth believed that only a properly trained and authorized priest could perform exorcisms, as they acted as instruments of God's grace in the battle against evil.
- **Psychiatric Evaluation:** Father Amorth was careful to differentiate between cases of true possession and mental illness. He emphasized the importance of a thorough

psychiatric evaluation to rule out any medical or psychological conditions before proceeding with an exorcism. He believed that a misdiagnosis could be harmful.

- **Collaboration with Medical Professionals:** Despite his strong belief in the supernatural, Father Amorth recognized the value of collaboration with medical professionals. He understood that some cases of apparent possession could be attributed to underlying medical conditions, and he encouraged a holistic approach to care.

- **Preventive Measures:** To prevent possession, Father Amorth emphasized the importance of living a virtuous and faith-filled life, participating in the sacraments of the Catholic Church, and avoiding any involvement with occult practices or sinful behavior.

- Father Gabriele Amorth's belief in the reality of demonic possession was an integral part of his faith and ministry as an exorcist. While his views were rooted in religious tradition, they also intersected with the broader discussions on the nature of evil, spirituality, and the supernatural in both religious and secular contexts.

- Father Amorth also believed in a hierarchy of demons, with Satan at the top. He claimed that some demons were more powerful and malevolent than others, and that their actions could vary in intensity.

- **Satan at the Top**: In Father Amorth's belief system, Satan, also known as the Devil or Lucifer, occupied the highest position in the demonic hierarchy. Satan is considered the embodiment of evil and is seen as the chief adversary of God and humanity.

- **Hierarchy of Demons:** Below Satan, Father Amorth believed in a hierarchy of demons that included various ranks and levels of malevolence. These demons were thought to be fallen angels who rebelled against God and followed Satan. They were believed to possess varying degrees of power and wickedness.

- **Different Demonic Ranks:** Father Amorth suggested that demons could be categorized into different ranks or orders. While there isn't a universally agreed-upon classification, traditional Christian demonology often includes categories such as principalities, powers, dominions, and minions. Each rank was thought to have its own distinct characteristics and abilities.

- **Varying Intensity of Actions:** According to Father Amorth's beliefs, the actions of demons could vary in intensity. Some demons were considered more powerful and influential than others, and they could potentially cause greater harm and suffering when they possessed or tormented individuals. These malevolent actions could range from spiritual oppression to possession.

- **Exorcism and the Battle Against Demons:** Father Amorth, as an exorcist, saw his role as combating these malevolent entities through exorcism rituals. He believed that by invoking the power of God and the Church, he could expel demons from possessed individuals, thereby freeing them from the influence and torment of these evil spirits.

It's important to note that Father Amorth's views on demonology were specific to his Catholic faith and not universally accepted within Christianity. Different religious traditions may have varying interpretations of the hierarchy of demons and the nature of spiritual warfare. Father Amorth's work as an exorcist brought attention to these beliefs and practices, sparking discussions and debates within and beyond the Catholic Church.

CHAPTER ELEVEN

THE LEGACY OF FATHER GABRIELE AMORTH

Father Gabriele Amorth is remembered for his profound impact on the world of exorcism and his tireless dedication to battling what he believed to be the forces of evil. Amorth's legacy extends beyond his religious ministry; it encompasses his commitment to providing spiritual guidance and comfort to countless individuals plagued by perceived demonic possession.

Amorth's career as an exorcist spanned several decades, during which he conducted thousands of exorcisms, earning him the title of the "Dean of Exorcists." His expertise and unwavering faith made him a sought-after figure, not only within the Catholic Church but also in popular culture. He demystified the process of exorcism, shedding light on its rituals and emphasizing the importance of distinguishing mental illness from demonic influence.

In addition to his hands-on exorcism work, Father Amorth authored numerous books on the subject, including "An Exorcist Tells His Story" and "An Exorcist: More Stories." These writings served as valuable resources for those interested in understanding the complexities of exorcism and the spiritual realm.

Amorth's legacy also includes his efforts to raise awareness about the existence of evil and the need for spiritual discernment in a modern world often skeptical of such matters. He firmly believed that the battle against malevolent forces was ongoing and that individuals needed spiritual guidance to navigate the challenges of life.

Despite facing criticism and skepticism, Father Gabriele Amorth remained steadfast in his beliefs and dedicated his life to assisting those who sought his help. His legacy continues to inspire discussions about faith, the supernatural, and the enduring human fascination with the unseen forces that shape our world. Father Amorth's contributions to the field of exorcism and his unwavering commitment to the spiritual well-being of others

ensure that his impact endures beyond his earthly
presence.

CHAPTER TWELVE

PERSONAL REFLECTIONS

Father Gabriele Amorth was a renowned Catholic priest and exorcist who dedicated his life to the study and practice of exorcism. In his personal reflections, he often emphasized the spiritual warfare he believed was at play in the battle against demonic possession. He contended that the devil actively sought to corrupt and control individuals, and it was the duty of the Church to confront this evil.

Amorth's reflections delved into the challenging and sometimes harrowing experiences he encountered during exorcisms. He expressed deep concern for those suffering from possession, describing their torment and the toll it took on their lives. Through his work, he sought to provide spiritual healing and relief to these afflicted individuals, viewing it as an act of compassion and service to God.

In addition to the spiritual aspect, Father Amorth also highlighted the importance of discernment and careful evaluation before proceeding with exorcisms. He stressed the need to distinguish between psychological issues and genuine cases of possession to ensure that the appropriate treatment was administered.

Father Gabriele Amorth's personal reflections reveal his unwavering dedication to his faith, his commitment to helping those in need, and his deep conviction in the reality of demonic possession as a spiritual battle. His work continues to be a subject of fascination and debate within the Catholic Church and the broader religious community.

CHAPTER THIRTEEN

THE FUTURE OF EXORCISM

The future of exorcism is a complex and multifaceted topic that encompasses various perspectives, including religious, cultural, and scientific viewpoints. While it's impossible to predict the exact trajectory of exorcism practices, we can explore some key trends and potential developments that may shape its future.

- **Evolution of Beliefs:** Exorcism is deeply rooted in religious beliefs and traditions. In the future, these beliefs may continue to evolve, leading to changes in the way exorcism is perceived and practiced within different faiths. Some religious communities may adapt their rituals or interpretations to align with modern sensibilities.

- **Interplay with Science:** As our understanding of mental health and psychology advances, there may be increased scrutiny and collaboration between religious practitioners and mental health professionals. Exorcism may be seen as a complementary or alternative approach to addressing psychological issues, with a greater emphasis on holistic well-being.

- **Technological Advances:** Technology could play a role in the future of exorcism. For instance, virtual exorcism sessions or online support groups may become more common. Additionally, advancements in brain-imaging and neurology may provide insights into the physiological aspects of possession experiences.
- **Globalization and Cultural Exchange:** As cultures continue to intermingle, the exchange of religious and spiritual practices will likely lead to cross-cultural influences on exorcism. This may result in hybrid rituals or new approaches to dealing with spiritual afflictions.
- **Legal and Ethical Considerations:** There may be increased scrutiny and regulation of exorcism practices, particularly concerning issues of consent and mental health. Ethical

guidelines and legal frameworks could emerge to ensure the well-being and rights of individuals undergoing exorcism.

- **Education and Training:** Religious institutions may offer more structured education and training for exorcists to ensure their competency and ethical conduct. This could lead to a more professionalized approach to exorcism.
- **Secularization:** In some societies, a trend toward secularization may reduce the prevalence of exorcism. As religious adherence declines, so too may the demand for exorcism services.
- **Alternative Spiritual Practices:** Some individuals may turn to alternative spiritual practices or New Age beliefs as alternatives to traditional exorcism. This could diversify the ways people seek spiritual solutions to life's challenges.

The future of exorcism is likely to be shaped by a combination of religious, cultural, scientific, and societal factors. How exorcism evolves will depend on the interplay of these influences and the willingness of religious institutions and practitioners to adapt to changing times and beliefs.

However Father Gabriele Amorth, who passed away in 2016, and dedicated much of his life to performing exorcisms and advocating for their continued practice within the Catholic Church hoped that exorcism would gain momentum in future through:

- **Recognition and Training:** Father Amorth hoped for a greater recognition of the need for exorcists within the Catholic Church. He believed that more priests should be trained in the rites of exorcism to meet the growing demand for spiritual help in dealing with cases of alleged demonic possession.
- **Openness and Understanding:** He aimed to reduce the stigma surrounding exorcisms and promote a better understanding of this practice within the Church and society at large. He emphasized that exorcisms were not just about driving out demons but also about providing spiritual support to individuals in distress.
- **Interfaith Dialogue:** Father Amorth was also open to interfaith dialogue on the subject of exorcism. He believed that different religious traditions could come together to

share insights and practices related to spiritual healing and deliverance from evil.

- **Increased Research:** He hoped that the Church would encourage more research into the field of demonology, possession, and related topics. This would involve collaborating with experts in psychology, psychiatry, and other relevant fields to better distinguish between genuine cases of possession and mental health issues.
- **Modernization of Exorcism Rites:** While he held traditional views on exorcism, Father Amorth acknowledged the need for updating the Church's exorcism rituals to address contemporary challenges and cultural contexts.

It's essential to note that the future of exorcism within the Catholic Church is influenced by various factors, including changes in the Church's leadership, evolving societal attitudes, and ongoing theological discussions. The direction it takes may differ from Father Amorth's hopes and aspirations, as opinions on this matter can vary among Church leaders and theologians.

Appendix

Glossary of Terms

- **Exorcism**: The religious ritual of expelling evil spirits or demons from a person or place.
- **Possession**: When an individual is believed to be under the control of a demonic entity or evil spirit.
- **Rite of Exorcism:** The prescribed religious ceremony performed by a trained exorcist to remove demonic influence.
- **Vatican**: The spiritual and administrative center of the Roman Catholic Church, located in Vatican City.
- **Demonology**: The study of demons and their characteristics, often associated with the practice of exorcism.

- **Catholic Church:** The worldwide Christian institution led by the Pope, which Father Gabriele Amorth served throughout his life.
- **Chief Exorcist:** Father Amorth's role within the Catholic Church, responsible for performing exorcisms and training other exorcists.
- **Spiritual Warfare:** The belief in the ongoing battle between good and evil forces in the spiritual realm.
- **Satanism:** The worship or veneration of Satan, often associated with demonic activities.
- **Faith:** A central theme in Father Amorth's life and work, referring to strong belief in God and the power of prayer.
- **Miracle**: Extraordinary events believed to be caused by divine intervention, sometimes associated with exorcisms.
- **Theology**: The study of the nature of God and religious belief, which informed Father Amorth's understanding of exorcism.
- **Catechism**: The official doctrine of the Catholic Church, containing teachings on faith and morality.

- **Pontifical University Regina Apostolorum:** The academic institution where Father Amorth studied and taught.
- **Psychiatry**: The branch of medicine dealing with mental illness, often intertwined with discussions about possession and exorcism.
- **Scepticism**: The attitude of questioning or doubting the reality of paranormal phenomena, which Father Amorth faced from some quarters.
- **Sacerdos**: The Latin term for priest, reflecting Father Amorth's role in the Church.
- **Legacy**: The lasting impact of Father Amorth's work on exorcism and spiritual guidance.
- **Pope John Paul II:** The influential Pope during Father Amorth's tenure as Chief Exorcist, with whom he had a close relationship.
- **Holy See:** The central governing body of the Catholic Church, responsible for establishing Church doctrine and policy.

These terms should help provide a deeper understanding of Father Gabriele Amorth's life and work within the context of the Catholic Church and the practice of exorcism.

Printed in Great Britain
by Amazon

34368839R00046